S0-BSV-939

DISCARDED
Valparaiso Public Library
Valparaiso, Jefferson Street
Valparaiso, IN 46383
Library System

Valparaiso - Porter County

The Greenwich Guide to the

Seasons

PORTER COUNTY LIBRARY

DISCARDED
Valparaiso-Porter County
Library System

Valparaiso Public Library
103 Jefferson Street
Valparaiso, IN 46383

DEC 13 2005

J NF   525.5 DOL   VAL
Dolan, Graham, 1953-
The Greenwich guide to the s
33410008559553

Heinemann Library
Chicago, Illinois

Graham Dolan

Royal Observatory Greenwich

Published by Heinemann Library,
an imprint of Reed Educational & Professional Publishing,
Chicago, IL
Customer Service 888-454-2279

Visit our website at www.heinemannlibrary.com

© National Maritime Museum 2001

All rights reserved. No part of this publication may be reproduced or transmitted in any form or by any means, electronic or mechanical, including photocopying, recording, taping, or any information storage and retrieval system, without permission in writing from the publisher.

Designed by Celia Floyd
Illustrations by Jeff Edwards
Originated by Dot Gradations
Printed in Hong Kong/China

05 04 03 02 01
10 9 8 7 6 5 4 3 2 1

Library of Congress Cataloging-in-Publication Data
Dolan, Graham, 1953-
  The seasons / Graham Dolan.
      p. cm. -- (The greenwich guide to)
Includes bibliographical references and index.
  ISBN 1-58810-044-8
  1. Seasons--Juvenile literature. [1. Seasons.] I. Title.
  QB637.4 .D66 2001
  525'.5--dc21

                                00-010542

Acknowledgments
The publisher would like to thank the following for permission to reproduce photographs: Still Pictures, p. 4; PhotoDisc, p. 5; National Maritime Museum, pp. 12, 13; Oxford Scientific Films, pp. 19, 26, 27; NHPA, p. 20; Bruce Coleman Collection, pp. 21, 23 top, 28, 29; Oxford Scientific Films, pp. 22, 23 bottom; Science Photo Library, pp. 24, 25.

Cover photograph reproduced with permission of PhotoDisc.

Spine logo reproduced with permission of the National Maritime Museum.

Every effort has been made to contact copyright holders of any material reproduced in this book. Any omissions will be rectified in subsequent printings if notice is given to the Publisher.

Some words are shown in bold, **like this.** You can find out what they mean by looking in the glossary.

Contents

The Seasons

In some parts of the world, the **year** consists of two seasons—a dry season and a rainy season. In central Australia, the Aborigines divide their year into five seasons. For most of us, though, the year is made up of four seasons: **spring, summer, autumn,** and **winter.**

The importance of the seasons

The things we do are influenced by the seasons. This was particularly true in the past, when more people were farmers and worked on the land. In spring, baby animals are born. Toward the end of the summer, wheat, corn, and other crops are harvested. In the autumn and winter, the fields are plowed and made ready for replanting.

Lambs are born in the spring.

When we go on vacation, where we go and what we do often depends on the time of year. We usually travel to the beach in the summer, when the weather is warmer. Skiing trips are usually taken in the winter, when the weather is colder and there is snow on the ground.

Many people go to the beach in the summer.

But why do the seasons occur? Why are they repeated from one year to the next? Why is it summer in Australia when it is winter in North America? The answers to these questions lie in the way in which Earth **orbits** the Sun.

Our Moving Earth

The Sun is our nearest star. It gives us light and **energy.**
Earth moves around the Sun. This movement, or **orbit,**
affects our **years,** seasons, and **days.**

As Earth goes on its journey, we pass from one season to
the next. The pattern of the seasons repeats itself each time
Earth begins a new orbit, which happens roughly every
$365\frac{1}{4}$ days. Our year is based on this repeating pattern.

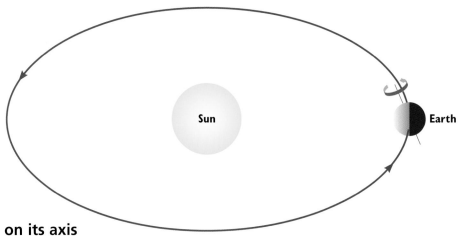

Earth spins on its axis
just over 365 times in the
time that it takes to orbit the Sun once.

Day and night

Earth is also spinning on its own **axis.** When the part of
Earth that we are on faces the Sun, we receive light and
energy. We call this **daytime.** As Earth spins, we eventually
end up facing away from the Sun. When this happens,
light and energy from the Sun can no longer reach us. It
gets dark, and **nighttime** begins.

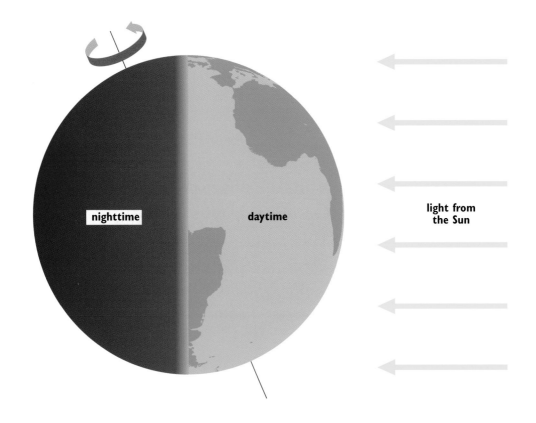

light from
the Sun

nighttime

daytime

**When it is daytime on
one side of Earth, it is
nighttime on the other.**

Long and short days

When we say that the days in **winter** are shorter than they
are in **summer,** we do not mean that the days themselves
are actually shorter. Each day is always 24 hours long.
What we mean is that there are fewer hours of daylight
each day and more hours of darkness. This happens
because Earth leans as it orbits the Sun.

Our Leaning Earth

As Earth makes its journey around the Sun, it leans at an angle on its **axis.** This affects the length of our **days** and the height at which the Sun appears in the sky. It causes the seasons to occur. Each end of Earth's axis is called a pole. The Earth has a North Pole and a South Pole.

As Earth moves around its **orbit,** the direction in which it leans stays about the same. On one side of its orbit, around June, Earth's North Pole points toward the Sun. On the opposite side of the orbit, around December, the North Pole points away from the Sun.

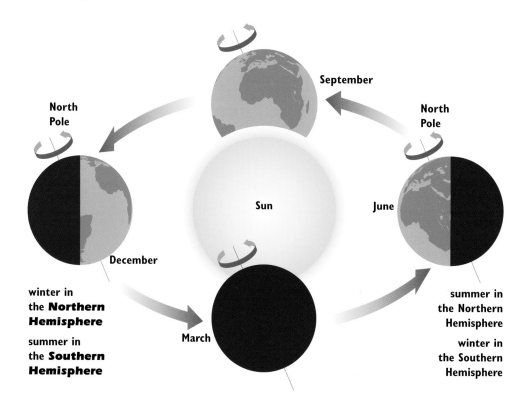

Earth always leans in the same direction as it orbits the Sun.

Summer and winter

When the North Pole points toward the Sun, people north of the **Tropics** get warmer weather. They have their **summer.** When the North Pole points toward the Sun, there are more hours of daylight each day, and the Sun rises higher in the sky. More **energy** is received, and it feels hotter. When the North Pole points away from the Sun, these people get colder weather. They have their **winter.**

In countries south of the Tropics, summer occurs when the South Pole points toward the Sun. This happens when the North Pole is pointing away from the Sun. Near the **equator,** the weather is warm most of the time.

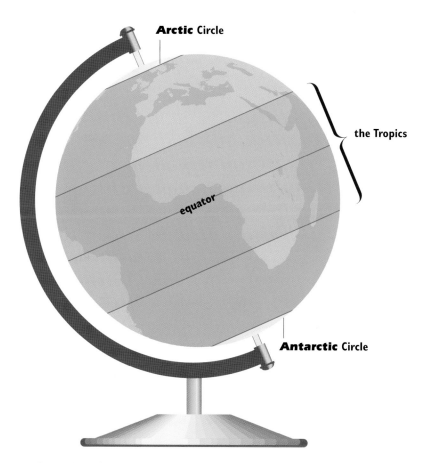

The area on each side of the equator is called the Tropics.

The Effect of Earth's Lean

The changing length of the day

In North America, the **days** are longer in the **summer,** because Earth is leaning on its **axis.** This part of Earth, in the **Northern Hemisphere,** spends more of the day facing toward the Sun than facing away from it. When days are longer, Earth receives more **energy** from the Sun, and the weather is hotter. In **winter,** this part of Earth spends more of the day facing away from the Sun than toward it. It receives less energy, and the weather is colder.

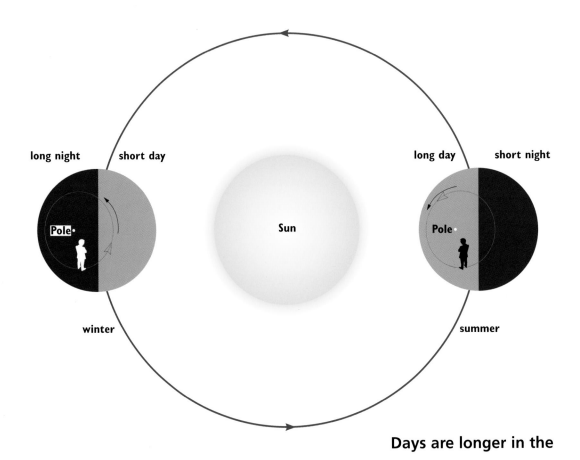

Days are longer in the summer than in the winter.

The height of the Sun

It also gets hotter in the summer because the Sun rises higher in the sky. This, too, is caused by Earth leaning on its axis. In summer, when the Sun rises high in the sky, its energy shines directly on Earth. Because Earth's surface gets lots of strong sunshine, the **temperatures** are warm. In winter, when the Sun is lower in the sky, its energy is spread out over a larger area of Earth's surface. Earth gets less sunshine, and the temperature drops to lower temperatures.

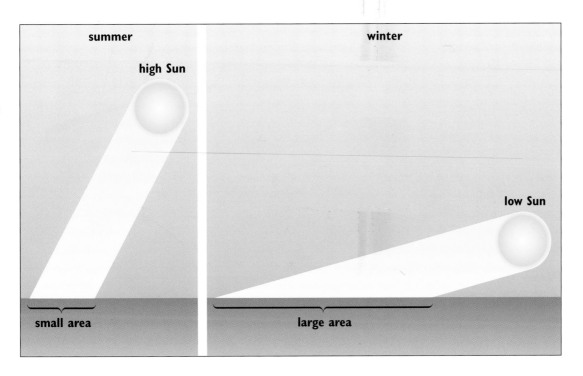

The midday Sun appears much higher in the sky in the summer than in the winter. When the Sun is lower, its energy is spread over a greater area. We get less of it, and the weather is colder.

The Four Seasons

Winter

In **winter**, the **midday** Sun is low in the sky. It is the time
of **year** when **temperatures** are usually at their lowest.
During the winter **months**, many trees lose their leaves,
and some animals **hibernate**.

In some places, snow is common in the winter. Other places
do not get cold enough for snow, even in the winter.

In some places, the appearance of daffodils marks the start of spring.

Spring

As Earth continues its journey around the Sun, the **days** rapidly become longer, and the Sun rises higher in the sky. Little by little, it starts to get warmer, and **spring** begins. The buds on trees start to open, and new leaves appear. Birds lay eggs that hatch a few weeks later.

Summer

In the **summer**, the days are at their longest, and the midday Sun is at its highest. Crops in the fields begin to ripen, and young birds leave their nests.

Autumn

In the **autumn**, the days quickly start to get shorter. The Sun does not rise as high in the sky, and the temperature begins to fall. Wild animals prepare themselves for the winter that will follow. The leaves of **deciduous trees** change color and fall to the ground.

13

The Length of Our Day

The length of our **day** depends on where we are and the time of **year**. On the **equator**, every day of the year has almost equal amounts of **daytime** and **nighttime**.

The farther north or south of the equator you are, the greater the difference between the amount of daytime in the **summer** and the amount of daytime in the **winter**.

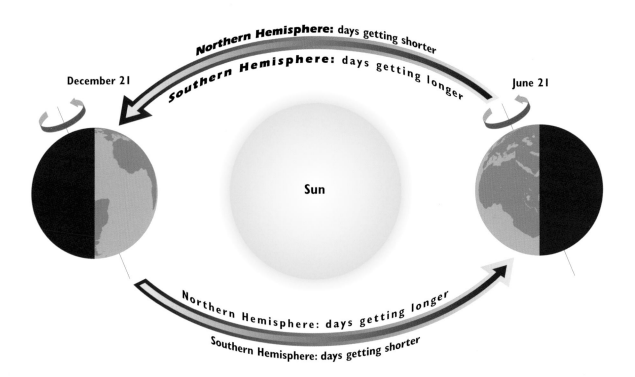

The length of our day changes as Earth orbits the Sun.

The Sun moves in different paths at different times of the year. This diagram shows how it moves in the United States and most of Europe.

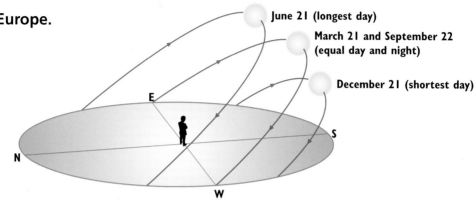

June 21 (longest day)

March 21 and September 22 (equal day and night)

December 21 (shortest day)

E

N

S

W

The longest and shortest days

The **longest** and **shortest days** of the year occur in June and December. The amount of daylight increases each day between the shortest and the longest day. It then starts to decrease again. Roughly halfway between the two, we get more or less equal amounts of daytime and nighttime.

Length of Day	Approximate Date	
	Northern Hemisphere (including North America)	*Southern Hemisphere* (including Australia)
Longest day	June 21	December 21
Shortest day	December 21	June 21
Equal day and night	September 22 and March 21	March 21 and September 22

The Seasons in the Arctic and Antarctic

Lands of midnight Sun

In the **Arctic** and **Antarctic** Circles, around the North and South Poles, there are long periods of unbroken darkness during the **winter.** In the **summer,** there are long periods of continuous daylight. The Sun is still in the sky at midnight. At the poles, there is about half a **year** of continuous **nighttime** followed by half a year of uninterrupted **daytime.** The number of **days** of each gets less as you move away from the poles.

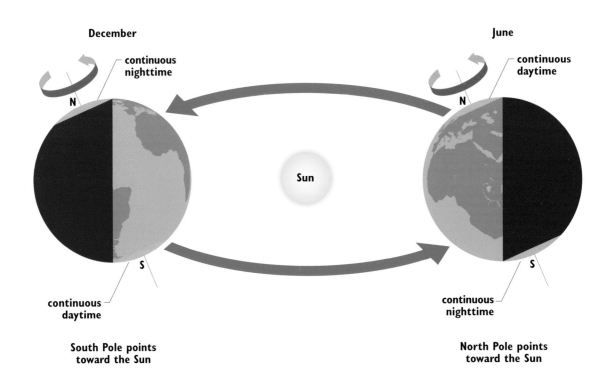

December

continuous
nighttime

N

Sun

S

continuous
daytime

**South Pole points
toward the Sun**

June

continuous
daytime

N

S

continuous
nighttime

**North Pole points
toward the Sun**

Cycles of daytime and nighttime are much longer at Earth's poles.

The circling polar Sun

At the poles, the Sun moves around the sky at virtually the same height from one day to the next. It moves in a spiral. At the North Pole, it spirals continuously upward until about June 21. It then starts to spiral downward again.

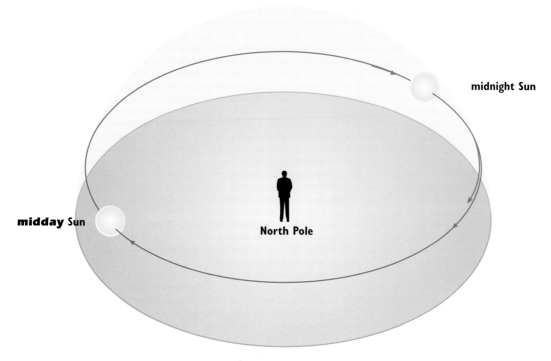

This is the upward path of the Sun at the North Pole in May.

The South Pole

At the South Pole, the average **temperature** in December, which is summertime there, is −18° Fahrenheit (−28° Celsius). That is colder than your freezer! Even so, it is much higher than the average temperature in June, during wintertime there, which is −72° Fahrenheit (−58° Celsius).

The Seasons Near the Equator

The absence of seasons

The four seasons of **spring**, **summer**, **autumn**, and **winter** do not occur near the **equator**. Here, there is very little difference in **temperature** from one **month** of the **year** to the next. This is because each **day** is about the same length, and the **midday** Sun is always high in the sky.

Location		Average temperature	
		Hottest month	Coldest month
equator	London, England	°Celsius 0 10 20 30 40 50 60 70 80 °Fahrenheit	°Celsius 0 10 20 30 40 50 60 70 80 °Fahrenheit
equator	Singapore	°Celsius 0 10 20 30 40 50 60 70 80 °Fahrenheit	°Celsius 0 10 20 30 40 50 60 70 80 °Fahrenheit
equator	Sydney, Australia	°Celsius 0 10 20 30 40 50 60 70 80 °Fahrenheit	°Celsius 0 10 20 30 40 50 60 70 80 °Fahrenheit

Rainy and dry seasons

In some places in the **Tropics**, there is a dry and a rainy season. Part of the year is drier than normal, and part of the year is wetter. In other parts of the Tropics, the rain falls more evenly throughout the year. The **climate** is influenced by the heating and cooling of the nearby land and oceans.

In the tropical rain forest, rain normally falls throughout the year.

Height of midday Sun		*Amount of **daytime** and **nighttime***	
Highest	Lowest	**Longest day**	**Shortest day**

19

Deciduous and Evergreen Trees

In the **Tropics**, trees usually keep their leaves all through the **year**. Trees like this are called **evergreen trees**. Beyond the Tropics, there is usually a mixture of evergreen and **deciduous trees**. Deciduous trees normally lose all their leaves in the **autumn** and grow new ones in the **spring**. The season of autumn is often called fall because of the many falling leaves.

Autumn colors

The leaves of deciduous trees change color before they fall to the ground in the autumn. The color they turn depends on the type of tree. Some turn red. Others turn yellow or brown. The brightness of the colors is affected by the **summer** and autumn weather. New England is particularly famous for its brightly colored autumn leaves.

The leaves of deciduous trees change color before they fall in autumn.

Evergreens in cold countries

The evergreen trees found in very cold places are usually **conifers.** Their leaves look like thin, spiky needles. Although evergreens with broad leaves are often able to survive in places with warmer **winters,** most are unable to survive the colder winters of the northern United States and Canada.

Woodland plants

Plants need light to grow. The ground in deciduous woodlands receives the most light in the early spring, when the trees have no leaves. This is when many woodland plants flower. In the summer, when there is a leaf **canopy** overhead, it is darker. Many woodland plants die back, surviving beneath the ground until growth starts again in the autumn.

Bluebells are woodland flowers. They bloom in late spring.

Hibernation and Migration

Hibernation

In the **winter,** there is less food around for wild animals. Some **mammals** survive the cold winters and the reduction in food supply by **hibernating.** In the **autumn,** when there is plenty of food, they fatten themselves up and store their **energy.** When they hibernate, they find a cozy place to settle for the winter. Their body **temperature** and heart rate drop. They use energy at a slower rate and are able to use their stored energy to live through the winter. To an outsider, they look as though they are asleep.

Dormice hibernate in the winter.

Migration

Some birds fly to a warmer place for the winter. This travel is called **migration**. Swallows, for example, spend the **summer** in northern Europe and the winter thousands of miles away in Africa, where it is warmer.

Fur color and length

In the winter, when it is colder, some mammals grow more and longer hair. In the summer, when it is warmer, they lose the extra hair. This is called **molting**. The color of the fur of some mammals also changes with the seasons. This helps them to stay **camouflaged** as the landscape around them changes.

Ermine have white fur in the winter to match the snow. In the summer, their fur changes to brown, and they are called stoats instead of ermine.

23

The Seasons on Other Planets

Most of the planets have seasons. The more a planet leans on its **axis** relative to its **orbit,** the greater the difference between its **summer** and **winter.** The planet that appears to lean the most is Uranus. It is almost lying on its side. The planet that leans the least is Mercury.

Planet	Tilt of axis
Mercury	0°
Venus	178°
Earth	24°
Mars	25°
Jupiter	3°
Saturn	27°
Uranus	98°
Neptune	30°
Pluto	122°

The planet Uranus spins on its side, causing a big difference between its summers and winters. Its blue-green color is caused by methane gas in the atmosphere.

Surface temperatures

Many other factors also affect the **climate** and weather patterns on the planets. These include the amount and type of **atmosphere** and the distance from the Sun. In general, the farther a planet is from the Sun, the colder its surface **temperature** is.

Small planets have less **gravity** and less atmosphere than larger ones. Mercury, the smallest of the inner planets, has almost no atmosphere. Mercury also does not lean on its axis. All its **days** are the same length, and there are no seasons.

The surface of Venus is permanently covered in clouds.

Venus is about the same size as Earth and has an atmosphere made up mainly of carbon dioxide. The carbon dioxide traps the Sun's **energy** and makes the planet hotter. As a result, the surface temperature on Venus is higher than on Mercury, even though it is farther from the Sun.

What If...?

... Earth was closer to the Sun?

If Earth was closer to the Sun, we would still have seasons, but **temperatures** would be higher. Earth would **orbit** the Sun more quickly. Our **years** would be shorter, and so would each of our seasons.

If we were close enough to the Sun, it would be too warm for water to freeze in the **winter**. The ice caps of the **Arctic** and **Antarctic** would not have formed, and the sea levels would be higher. If we were any closer than that, it would be too hot for life as we know it to exist.

These ice caps would melt if Earth were closer to the Sun.

If Earth did not lean, there would be no deciduous trees. Trees would keep their leaves throughout the year because the temperature would be about the same in December as in June.

... Earth did not lean?

If Earth did not lean, we would not have seasons. And if we did not have the seasons, we probably would not measure time in years, either. Our longest unit of time would be the **month.** The length of each month is based on the time it takes for the Moon to orbit Earth.

If there were no seasons, there would be no **deciduous trees.** All the trees would be **evergreens.**

If Earth did not lean, the **midday** Sun would always reach the same height in the sky. Each **day** would be much like any other day. Every day would have about the same amount of **daytime** as **nighttime.** The farther away from the **equator** you were, the cooler it would be.

Fact File

Long school vacations in the **summer** began in the past, when children helped to collect the harvest.

The highest **temperature** ever recorded on Earth's surface, in the shade, was 136° Fahrenheit (58° Celsius). The lowest temperature ever recorded was −129° Fahrenheit (−89.4° Celsius).

In Yakutsk, Russia, the difference between the highest recorded summer temperature and the lowest recorded **winter** temperature is 115° Fahrenheit (64° Celsius).

In Murmansk, Russia, the largest town north of the **Arctic** Circle, the Sun does not set for about 62 **days** in a row during the summer.

Arctic ground squirrels **hibernate** for nine **months** of the **year.** This helps them survive the long, cold winter without having to go out in search of food.

The arctic ground squirrel hibernates to avoid the cold.

The coldest place where people live year-round is the village of Oymyakon in Russia, where the temperature has fallen below –96° Fahrenheit (–71° Celsius).

About one-tenth of Earth's land is permanently covered in ice. It stays frozen even in the summer months.

Around March 21 and September 22, the **midday** Sun passes directly overhead at the **equator.**

The seasons on Mars last roughly twice as long as those on Earth. Mars is farther from the Sun, so it takes longer to complete each **orbit.**

The body temperature of snakes and other reptiles is higher in the summer than in the winter.

Garden plants that are able to survive the cold weather and frosts in the winter are called hardy plants.

Once a tree has been cut down, you can guess its age by counting the number of tree rings. It has one for each year of its life. The rings form because trees grow at different rates in different seasons.

Tree rings show the age of a tree.

Glossary

Antarctic   part of Earth near the South Pole

Arctic   part of Earth near the North Pole

atmosphere   layer of gases that surrounds a planet. A planet's atmosphere affects its temperature and weather.

autumn   season between summer and winter, also called fall

axis   imaginary line passing through the center of a planet from the North to the South Pole, around which the planet spins

camouflage   to blend in with the surrounding area, often by changing color

canopy   covering of something

climate   general type of weather and temperatures that a place experiences

conifer   evergreen tree, like a pine or fir tree, that has needles and cones

day   length of time based on the time it takes for Earth to spin around once on its axis

daytime   time between sunrise and sunset

deciduous tree   tree that loses all its leaves in the autumn and grows new ones in the spring

energy   what it takes to heat something up or to make it move

equator   imaginary line that separates Earth's Northern and Southern Hemispheres

evergreen tree   tree that keeps its leaves throughout the year

gravity   force that attracts objects to each other. Earth's gravity gives us our weight and holds Earth's atmosphere in place.

hibernate   to spend the winter in an inactive state

longest day   day in the year with the most hours and minutes of daytime

mammal   warm-blooded animal that feeds its young with milk produced by the mother; class of animal that includes humans

midday   time when the Sun reaches its highest point of the day

migration   moving from one place to another

molting   shedding of hair in the spring and summer

month length of time based on the time it takes for the Moon to orbit Earth once

nighttime time between sunset and sunrise

Northern Hemisphere half of Earth north of the equator

orbit path of a planet around the Sun, or of a moon around a planet

shortest day day in the year with the fewest hours and minutes of daytime

Southern Hemisphere half of Earth south of the equator

spring season between winter and summer

summer hottest part of the year, when the days are longest and the Sun rises highest in the sky

temperature how hot or cold something is

Tropics part of Earth near the equator between the tropic of Cancer and the tropic of Capricorn

winter coldest part of the year, when the days are shortest and the Sun is always low in the sky

year length of time based on the time taken for Earth to orbit the Sun once and for the cycle of seasons to repeat itself. A normal calendar year has 365 days. A leap year has 366 days.

More Books to Read

Burton, Jane and Kim Taylor. *The Nature & Science of Autumn.* Milwaukee, Wis.: Gareth Stevens Inc., 1999.

Burton, Jane and Kim Taylor. *The Nature & Science of Spring.* Milwaukee, Wis.: Gareth Stevens Inc., 1999.

Burton, Jane and Kim Taylor. *The Nature & Science of Summer.* Milwaukee, Wis.: Gareth Stevens Inc., 1999.

Burton, Jane and Kim Taylor. *The Nature & Science of Winter.* Milwaukee, Wis.: Gareth Stevens Inc., 1999.

Hunter, Rebecca M. *The Seasons.* Austin, Tex.: Raintree-Steck-Vaughn Publishers, 2001.

Index